THE STORY-TELLING COTTAGE
by Nora Mogielski

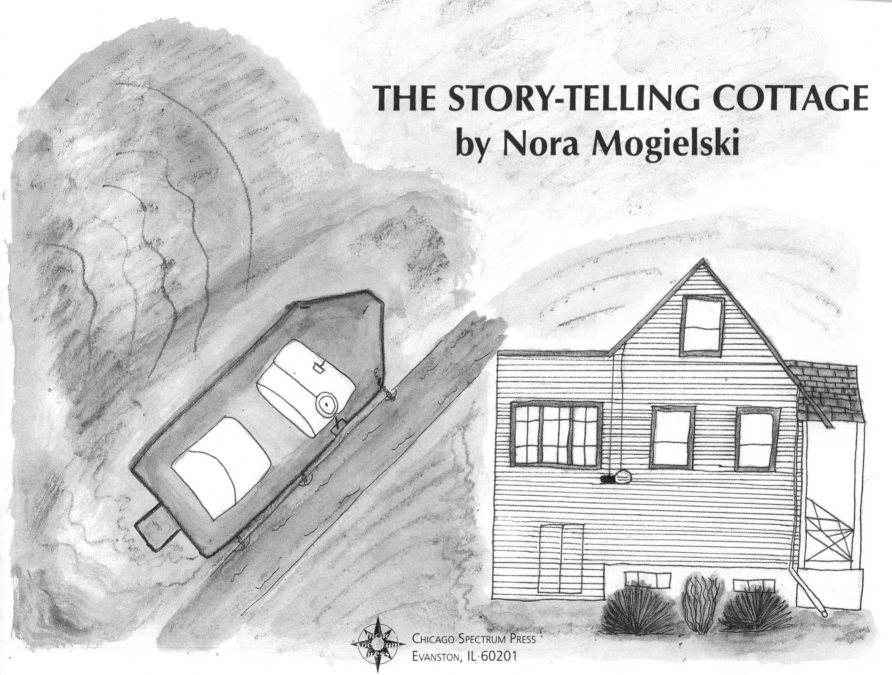

CHICAGO·SPECTRUM PRESS
EVANSTON, IL·60201

CHICAGO SPECTRUM PRESS
1571 SHERMAN AVENUE
EVANSTON, IL 60201
1-800-594-5190

Printed in the U.S.A.

10 9 8 7 6 5 4 3 2 1

ISBN: 1-886094-55-1

To order additional copies of this book, contact:

Roots & Wings, Inc.
8333 Antioch Road
Box 0386
Salem, WI 53168
414-843-4582

To Lisa,
Share your stories
& Live your dreams.
Thanks for sharing your
insight with me.
Love, Nora Mogielski
11/97

DEDICATION

To Phyllis Seno Iovino, my grandmother, for showing me what determination, humor, and wit can achieve.

To all my cousins, who loved the cottage as much as I did. It was a place where we didn't have to be anything but ourselves.

To Cara, Lauren, and Alyssa, who just started getting familiar with the cottage.

To you, grandparents and grandchildren, so that you may really get to know each other and share your stories.

The cottage is a house located in Southeastern Wisconsin. It is on Center Lake.

My grandparents, Phyllis and Gabriel, built it forty-five years ago when they were raising a family.

The cottage had three bedrooms and no closets.

My grandfather, who was born in Naples, Italy, grew up putting his clothes in large dressers called "Armoires," instead of closets.

My cousins and I liked the attic. It had wall to wall beds, and of course, no closets.

We would go up there to sleep but we would stay up late to laugh, sing, dance and tell stories. It hasn't been like that for a long time because many of us are now grown-up.

I'm staying with my grandmother this weekend to help her clean up the cottage. My grandmother was born in December, 1910. She is a widow, which means that her husband, my grandfather, died many years ago.

As we walked through the kitchen, Grandma looked around. This was her favorite cooking space. She used to make the best tasting pasta here.

She wore an apron in this kitchen and cooked for everyone who came here.

Sometimes I helped her knead
dough to make bread. She
wrapped it with a white towel to
help it rise.

She baked the bread in her old-fashioned oven in her kitchen.

Now, Grandma walked to her favorite green chair in the living room. She would sit there with the screen door open and watch television while she crocheted Afghan blankets.

This warm summer day, Grandma
struggled with the decision
to sell the cottage, but knew it had
to be done.

She remembered all the happiness that
took place in this house.

While she sat in her chair
with toast and coffee beside
her, she began to dream . . .

She began to dream of another place in time.

A breeze blew through the door to give her fresh air. Outside, the sun shown brightly while birds chirped their favorite songs.

In the driveway, trucks and cars
pulled in to start moving furniture.

Moving

And Grandma remembered planting corn, tomatoes, green peppers, and flowers in the garden. She tended those plants carefully.

She tied white rags around sticks to keep the leaves off the ground. She always had a good crop.

People gathered in the yard.

18

Grandma dreamed of making jelly with the grapes from the grapevine. Her hair was pinned up in a scarf and she had on her apron again.

I would get a big bushel basket and cut the grapes off the vine for her to use.

While voices said hello to each other under the grapevine . . .

Grandma dreamed on about her five children and fifteen grandchildren playing around the cottage.

Now she also has twenty great-grandchildren and three great-great-grandchildren. They call her "Nani."

Outside the cottage, everyone stood around the seawall looking at the water. They felt just as sad as Grandma about selling the cottage.

My grandfather had written all of our names in the concrete of the seawall.

Grandma remembered painting the porch. Her children had been upset because they wanted her to relax more and take it easy.

As I sat on the porch watching her nap, I thought about the other relatives who wanted to buy the cottage. Grandma was the keeper of this house. Without her, it would lose its shape. She was the one who patta-pat-patted the babies and sang to them. She was the one who told stories of her childhood, and her marriage, and her vacations. She was the soul maker of this house.

All the aunts and uncles visited and
played cards. The cousins fished,
water skied, or played ball.

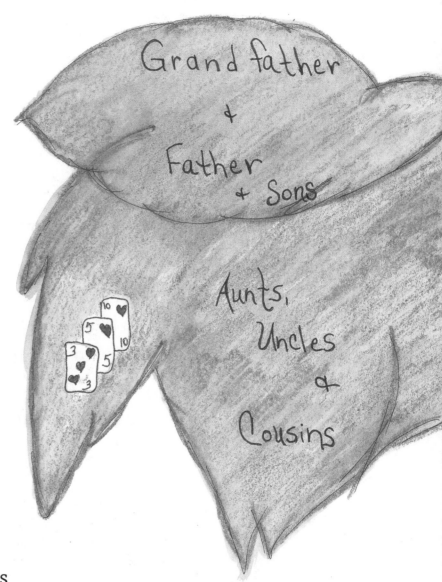

They had so much fun, they got wild. Grandma was
the keeper of the wild things.

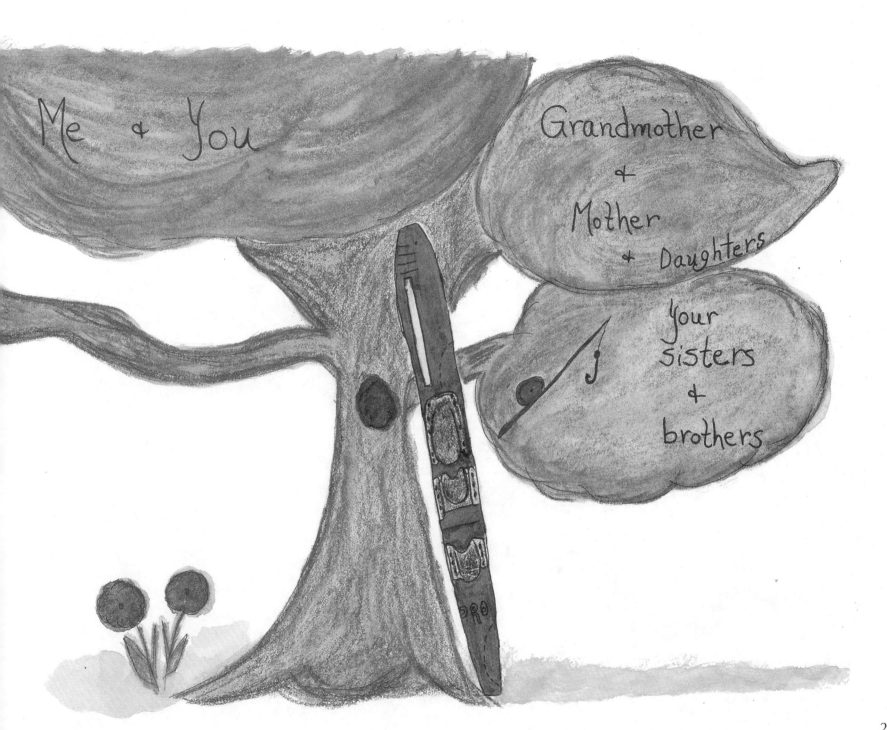

Me & You

Grandmother
&
Mother
& Daughters

Your
sisters
&
brothers

Grandma had given some of us the key to
the cottage, but she will always be the
key-holder.

Now, Grandma awoke to nearby sounds. Her eyesight was not that good, her bones ached sometimes, and she used a cane.

She could barely get out of her chair. I walked over to kiss her and help her get up.

"I see you brought your camera," she said.

"The cottage was always here, a part of us. We don't have many pictures. We need something to remember," I said.

"It will always be a part of us. It will linger in our hearts," said Grandma, as she reached out to hold my arm.

"Yes, Grandma, it will," I said as we walked out to greet some of the relatives.

Comments from special readers:

"I like the names on the seawall." .... Jaimie Wegel, age six

"Grandpa is a Packer fan. My grandpa is my dad's dad." .... Alex Philipps, age four

"I like the names on the bricks and I like to visit my grandma." .... John McEntegart, age six

"I like this story because it is my great-grandma." .... Alyssa Rosch, age five

"I have two grandmas." .... Royce Shippee, age four

"I like to go on walks with Grandma." .... Emma Shippee, age five

"I like to color at Grandma's." .... Kristofer Edmonds, age five

"I play Nintendo with Grandpa." .... Ismael Morales, age four

"I have two grandmas and I like my Grandpa." .... Michael Neurauter, age four

"I love you Ms. Nora." .... Eric Idler, age four

"My favorite part is Grandma's dreaming" .... Nick O'Brien, age six

"The children dancing around the attic is my favorite part.
The story reminds me of my grandma. She died on a Monday
in January, last year." .... Chelsea VanAken, age seven

"I like the picture of the attic because there is a lot of little
pictures and it is colorful. That was my favorite room
in the house." .... Lauren Rosch, age six

"It reminds me of how children get to do other things at
their grandparents that they don't get to do at home. I used
to play in my grandparent's attic." .... Cathy McKinnon, age fifteen

"I like the attic picture and baking picture because I like
to sing, dance, and bake." .... Cara Rosch, age eight